He Kissed Me

Stacey,
Merry Christmas!
May God continue to
bless and keep you.
Tara L.

He Kissed Me

POETIC WORSHIP

Tara D. Lewis

AuthorHouse™
1663 Liberty Drive
Bloomington, IN 47403
www.authorhouse.com
Phone: 1-800-839-8640

© 2011 by Tara D. Lewis. All rights reserved.

No part of this book may be reproduced, stored in a retrieval system, or transmitted by any means without the written permission of the author.

First published by AuthorHouse   08/19/2011

ISBN: 978-1-4634-4912-4 (sc)
ISBN: 978-1-4634-4911-7 (ebk)

Library of Congress Control Number: 2011914184

Printed in the United States of America

Any people depicted in stock imagery provided by Thinkstock are models, and such images are being used for illustrative purposes only.
Certain stock imagery © Thinkstock.

This book is printed on acid-free paper.

Because of the dynamic nature of the Internet, any web addresses or links contained in this book may have changed since publication and may no longer be valid. The views expressed in this work are solely those of the author and do not necessarily reflect the views of the publisher, and the publisher hereby disclaims any responsibility for them.

Contents

Here I Am To Worship 1
   Deliverance 2
   The Day Will Come 3
   Understanding 5
   I Love You Lord 7
   He Kissed Me 9
   Lord I Simply Come 12
   Morning Worship Makes the Difference 14
   Never Has Life 17
   Thank You Lord Blues 19
   Lift of a Wing 21
Here I Am To Listen 25
   Be Still 26
   Purpose 28
   Patiently 30
   God is God 32
   Stone Pillar of Light 33
   Standing Against the Darkness 35
   New Season 37
   The Gathering 39
   Now is the Time 41

Send Me 43
    What Would You Have Me To Do 44
    Come 46
    Expectation 48
    Prepare Me 49
    Another Level 51
    I've Come Too Far 53
    Use Me 55
    Got To Tell It (The News) 56
    Listen—Then Go 57

For Imani

Dreams do come true

*My heart is overflowing with a good theme.
I recite my composition concerning the king;
my tongue is the pen of a ready writer.
Psalms 45:1 NKJ*

Here I Am To Worship

Deliverance

My Lord
I come to You as humble as I know how
Lord, my life has gone through some changes
And not for the good
I seem to find myself
Caught up in man
Caught up in evil
Every which way I turn
Destruction and sorrow follow
It consumes all that I do
Lord, I can't take it anymore
You said ask
Lord, I ask for deliverance

The Day Will Come

The day will come
When gray days will come undone
And joy will prevail in the morning light

My love, pure and true
Will be like sun rays breaking through the clouds
Anxious to fill your world with light

The day will come
When flowers will empty their sweet nectar
Into the sun kissed air
And you, ensnared, will come

Drawn like a bee
Slowly indulging in the nourishment I provide
Humming your earthy song

The day will come
When the harmony of the wind, melody of the beast,
Base line of our hearts
Will become hazy, fade, and disappear

Only then can my light and your music find the other
And the song we sing
Will be of our own creation

The day will come
When our song will be perfected
And we will be that which we were created to be

Together, as one
We shall present our song, a new song
To He that said it would be
Bowed down on bended knee

Understanding

I don't always understand
Just how I fit in Your plan
Or why You saw fit
To make me Yours

I don't always know
Why it is You love me so
How You take me back
When I fail

There have been times
When I almost wished
You wouldn't care
Then I could wallow
Swallow my despair
And sink into my shame
But You ignored my half hearted plea
Gave me strength, hope, joy
Told me to come on

Lord, I just don't know
Even those moments

My actions said turn form me
My heart filled to overflowing
With love for You and pain for my actions

You've brought me out of more dark places
Than my friends will ever know
And I thank You for those times
But I praise You for being my God
And looking at my heart and not my actions

Lord, I'm steady struggling
To find just where I belong
To be consistent in character
An example of Christ

All that I am is Yours
Though I don't always understand
I'll continue to yield my will
And look for that
Great getting up morning
To see Your face and understand

I Love You Lord

I love You Lord
In my own special way
And the life I live
Is for Your glory

The day breaks
And the sun shines my way
All I can think
Is how You've blessed me
To start all over again

Today I'll praise You more
Your word shall nourish me
My prayers will never cease

I love You Lord
In my own special way
And the life I live
Is for Your glory

My soul cries out to thee
Hallelujah

Tara D. Lewis

My mouth fills with Your praise
Hallelujah

Lord I praise You
And I lift You up
Higher, Higher, Higher

I love You Lord
In my own special way
And the life I live
Is for Your glory

He Kissed Me

Asleep for half an eternity
I waited for that smile
Longed for that touch
Eager to be awakened and take part

As I slept
Dreams danced about
Leading me deeper into the abyss
Colorful and fast paced were they
Always insisting
On taking me to play hide and seek
Never did I have a chance
To seek
Bound was I to hide
Hide in my own dream
Leaving me fatigued and on edge

But somewhere
In my secret place
Where fast passed dreams try to invade
I found a semblance of peace
I rested

I longed to wake
And end the tormenting delight
Oh, how I waited
For my Prince Charming
To rescue me with a kiss of life

For half an eternity
I lay tormented
In this sweet abyss
Always dodging
Always running
Always
Never
Finding that nurturing warmth
Frustrated
I turned to my secret place
And said "I'm tired!"

Peace! Where are you?
Joy! When did you leave?
Love! Were you ever mine?
My prince
Why have you left me here so long?
I want to know
The Peace
In Your arms
The Joy
In Your eyes
The Love

He Kissed Me

In Your heart
I want You
Jesus

White lights danced about me
A warmth filled the empty space
Peace, Joy, and Love
Came flooding in
Then I saw His smile
He kissed me

Lord I Simply Come

Lord, I come humbly before You
I come to seek Your face
In the midst I adore You
Lord, I simply come

Devesting myself of sin
That would clothe me with burdens
I cast all my cares at Your feet
Here, I come humbled by Your truth
Leaving the world behind

Entering into our secret place
My desire is to seek Your face
Come into Your presence
Climb in Your arms and inquire of You

My heart fills and overflows with Your love
My arms rise and swirl above me
In perfect time to my feet
That beat beat beat beneath me
My voice caries the endearing praise

That's upon my lips
An offering

"Hallelujah! Hallelujah!
To God be the Glory
He reigns forever more
For He alone has kept me
He alone has met me
In every season
Hallelujah! Hallelujah!"

Lord, I come
I simply come

Morning Worship Makes the Difference

Morning worship makes the difference
And this I well do know
For one beautiful sun bright morning
I woke up and looked towards my day
I knew in an instant that I needed to pray
Off I went to be alone with God

I told Him I loved Him
And we talked, laughed, and I cried
I praised Him with songs
Sweet and straight from the heart
I fed upon His word
And He quenched my thirst with His spirit

"Holy, Holy, Holy is thy name, Oh Lord
Holy is Thy name
Your praises I shall continue to lift
Higher and higher
Holy is Thy name"

He Kissed Me

Joy fell upon my heart
A smile crept up to my face
Love for the world and all God's creations
Flowed freely from within me

Conquer all things could I
For God was truly with me
Watching and guiding my every step
And holding me tenderly near

When obstacles would try to trip me
I would say "In Jesus name be thou removed"
And continue to walk along my designated path
Free, clear, and true

Nothing not of God could stand against me
For I had remembered my time in the morning
And smiled as I praised Him
Everything I needed for victory
Were there where they belonged

So filled was I on feeling good
I did not stop to say good night
To Jesus who made my day
Oh, how fitfully I slept that night

Upon rising the next morning
I rushed pass God to get right into my day
Without talking things over and taking it His way

Soon as I hit the day
Fear settled upon me
I tried to shake it off
It wouldn't go
And poor me forgot what words to say

I prayed a vain prayer
And sang a vain song
Fear hung in there truly strong

Oh, my spirit groaned and groaned
Doubling over inside
Ah, I had to get rid of the fear
It was paralyzing me
So, I went back to the One I forsook that morning
"Lord, Jesus, forgive me…"

Never Has Life

Never has life been completely dark
There has always been a light
Showing me the safer places to step
Every now and then my eyes would wonder
My feet would fall in the shadows
And the darkness would bear down

Why didn't someone tell me
That Jesus had prayed for me
That the love I have was given
Before I knew what it was

One lonely night the shadows devoured my walls
And the nightmares of life stepped in to beat me down
Down I went on bent knees seeking out my light
When Jesus' ray fell upon my heart
God's word did call
And what should I read but that Jesus prayed for me
That I should love, be loved, prefect, and complete

Tara D. Lewis

Why didn't someone tell me
That Jesus had prayed for me
That the love I have was given
Before I knew what it was

Thank You Lord Blues

I don't need your pity, Baby
I've got my faith higher bound
Said, I don't need your pity, Baby
To drag my soul deep into the ground
If you want to help me, Baby
Send up a prayer that I'll be found

I was walking all alone
Or so I thought
Playing devil games
In the dead of dark
Trouble and heartache
Became my maiden name
Till the Lord grabbed my soul
And shook
And shook
And shook

I don't need your pity, Baby
I've seen the wrong in my life
Said, I don't need your pity, Baby
To make everything alright

If you feel you gota do something, Baby
Thank the Lord you weren't born in this sin'n town

One by one
The devil's hooks fell
In a singe of burnt desire
I looked up and saw an angel
Standing in the purest light
I fell on my knees
Crying Jesus
Oh Jesus
Thank You
Thank You, Jesus

I don't need your pity, Baby
I've got my soul in order
Said, I don't need your pity, Baby
To drag me back to sin
If you want to do right by me
Praise the Lord that I've been freed

Lift of a Wing

With the lift of a wing
And a step towards the sky
A bird takes flight
As the wind cuddles him
In the safety net of her arms
And shows him the Glory
Excited with joy and thanksgiving
The bird lets go of winds arm
And dances about God's blue bosom
Singing sweet praises to the heart
God in His loving compassion
Looks upon the bird and says "Eat"
With the same exuberance with which he sang
He dives into stagnant water
And partakes of God's goodness
Just before the bird takes hold of his meal
He whispers to the stagnant water
"Wake up. You're in the presence of God"
"I know" cries the stagnant water
"But what should I do? What does He want?"
"Listen" whispers the wind
"Listen to His word which I carry to those who'll hear.

Many times I have brought His word to you
But you wished to be deaf.
I watched as your water became murky then stagnant.
Now perhaps you will hear."
The wind blew gently across the stagnant water
And the water rippled
As it listened to the word of God
Storm clouds filled the sky
Thunder and lightening ripped it to shreds
As the sun and moon took turns adorning it
The water began to believe
"Glory" cried the water
The mud began to clear up
Trash was pushed away
Grass perked up at its cry
And turned green with expectation
Trees sent their roots to investigate
Then the roots began to run towards the water
When the roots touched the water
They sent forth a mighty ripple
The name of Jesus vibrated throughout the water
It was absorbed
Then reflected towards the world
And the water cried and spewed forth his tears
As each tear came forth
It was caught up
Above the ripple
And was given a new life in the sun
To celebrate the tears came together

He Kissed Me

And began to dance above the water
As they moved upon the word of God
That steadily rippled the water
The birds lifted their voices
In the air and in the treetops
The wind whistled as it danced
With the birds of the sky
Then they all looked towards the shore
Water with its dancing tears
Gestured for the shore to join in the celebration
It does
Sacrificing its sand
And the water it tears
They come together with a joyful shout
To give God the glory in a new song of praise
Now what was once stagnant is simply still
Hallelujah!

Here I Am To Listen

Be Still

(Psalm 46:10-11)

Be still and know that I am God
Be still
Be still
And know that I am God

The earth applauds as My presence fills the temple
The heavens rejoice at the sound of my name
The foundations I laid from beginning to end
I am God
Be still for I am God

The very hair on your head I've counted
Time and time again
I see your future and know your past
Believe it
Right here and now is where I want you to stand

Stand upon My word
Stand within My grace
Stand for the coming of your king
Be still and know that I am God

Be still and know that I am God
Be still
Be still
And know that I am God

I am God
The Alpha and Omega
I am God
The beginning and the end
I am God
The crucified and risen Lord
I am the Great I Am

So when the worries of life surround you
And it seems as though you can't find your way
Through the pressure at work and turmoil at home
Come to Me
And I will give you rest
Take My yoke upon you
Learn from Me
For I am gentle and lowly in heart
And you will find rest

Be still and know that I am God
Be still
Be still
And know that I am God

Purpose
(Esther 4:16)

From the beginning I created you from the dust
    Formed and fashioned you in My image

In the womb I dwelt with you
    Laid hands upon you
    Chose you

At your birth I called you
    And placed a mantel of bittersweet destiny
    At the time a mantel to big and heavy laden

Over the years you've struggled with that mantel
Some days it seemed so heavy and long
It held you back
Other days you wondered
Just why you could not take it off

But with each trial and tribulation that mantel
    Seemed to shrink and get a little lighter
But that was only you getting bigger and stronger

Now it seems as though
That mantel has been tailor made
And before you stands the door (wide open)
    To which you've been heading
    Your purpose

Pull that mantel tight around you and walk through

For I've called you for such a time as this

Patiently

That moment before your conception
I called you MY child
Embraced you within Me
Then sent you on a journey of great love

My heart arched when you were born
But I had need to sacrifice you
I knew (and still know)
Of your greatness—power

Patiently
I watched
My heart bled—you turned from Me
Still patiently—you Are My Child—I stood
And kept my eye upon thee

Yes, I saw all
That you endured
Felt your pain
Agonized when this world
Brutalized you
But I had need to sacrifice you

He Kissed Me

Patiently—I waited
As you struggled
Against those things
Which you were ignorant of
I waited
For your blind eye to see
And your deaf ears of hear

Often when you were alone
And at your lowest
I would wrap My Spirit around thee
And whisper-
Seek Me, My love is greater.
Seek Me, My love is greater.
I had need for you

Patiently I waited
For the day you would
Stand tall before principalities
Powers, rulers of darkness
And declare My name
And accept your inheritance

Oh, yes, I had need to sacrifice you
And wait patiently
For you to answer My first call
My beacon through the darkness
My light

God is God

God is hearing
God is moving
And He is answering your prayer

He is merciful
He is gracious
He is God
And He hears and answers your prayers

No matter how much stress
And the test you must endure
God is God
And He hears and answers your prayers

So lift up your eyes to Zion
Stretch forth thy hands towards heaven
Cry with a loud voice
And know that
God is God
And He hears and answers your prayers

Stone Pillar of Light

Despise not your years
For they are a blessing
Many have come and gone
But you stand strong
My Stone
I've placed you here
As a witness of My word
Just as Joshua placed the stone under the oak
Should the people deny Me

It's not by chance
That you are still here
For I've set you as pillars
In your family, church, and community
It is to you people look
For guidance, direction, and strength
You stand as a monument to Me
Of the great things I've done

Don't think that you are not seen
Your light shines brighter
Because of your testimony

Your light has drawn many
Out of darkness and into My waiting arms

Be not discouraged or dismayed
For I continue to be with you
My Stone Pillar of Light

Standing Against the Darkness

He is out here in this void
Seeking to destroy my life
My hands feel bound—My tongue seems numb
I almost fear for my life
Then I hear the spirit of God say
"Stand! Show forth your light."

Much time has passed and I'm still standing
Here in this filthy place
If I moved an inch I would touch the darkness
Lord, I'm still here—Just standing
Right here, in front of me is the accuser
I can smell his wretched breath with each word that he utters

> Agggh . . . I'm not listening to you
> I'm not tired or scared
> No, I won't give up
> You can't have me
> My God has not forsaken me—not here

But I'm still standing
Just as I feel I can no longer sustain my weight
I feel the spirit of God and in the distance
I hear a hum that turns into a loud rumble

Hallelujah for the saints that pray
Who take heed to the spirit of God
Thank you Jesus for the place
Where they intercede for all

Though the darkness is about me
I can feel your prayers
Though it tries to suffocate me
I can hear your prayers
With each bent knee, uplifted hand, and humble heart
I feel my help and strength
I can still see the accuser but I can no longer hear him
Just the sweet glorious sound of prayers

Yes, Holy is the Lamb
That was slain for the sins of the world
Holy is the Lord God Jehovah
God alone will be exalted
In the heavens and in the earth
And God alone will be exalted
Here in the depths of despair
Where I stand and show forth my light
Hallelujah

New Season

Who said life would be easy?
You have faced your share of giants
Some of them you defeated
Others you simply wounded
Yet you are still standing

Don't just stand there
Shake yourself
Look around
One season has ended

It's a new season!
New opportunities
New blessings
New people
And yes, new giants

So, let go of the old
"Behold I do a new thing"
Are you ready?

Tara D. Lewis

Then walk boldly into this
New season
And know you are where
You are suppose to be

The Gathering

I stumbled upon a gathering
Of people claiming and proclaiming the faith
Living high on hauteur as they looked down on me

My clothes are tattered
My hair could use a trim
For all these things I can truthfully say
I am clean within

The ladies cloaked in beauty cower behind the men
As they stiffen in fright
But there was one kindly man who held out a hand
And drew me in

Slowly the tension eased and the discussion resumed
As I sat listening
To profound declarations of righteousness
By all but the kindly man

As time was added then multiplied

Animation grew
Facades began to slip
Anger and pride revealed themselves

Scratching my head
I tried hard to figure out
If all this talk was about Jesus
What was the argument about

I turned to the kindly man and asked
If we are one with Jesus and He with us
And if the love we have for Jesus
Is the same love we have for our brothers
Why do these people feel the need to argue

The kindly man took me by my hand and said
My brother I do not know

Now is the Time

Now is the time to wake up
The shofar is sounding
Now is the time to get up
The enemy has set his trap
Now is the time to move
And position yourself
Now is the time
To be
To do
To say
All that God commands

Where are my spiritual warriors?
Now is the time
Please stand up

Send Me

What Would You Have Me To Do

What will You have me to do today
What word shall I speak
What path should I take
What would You have me to do

I recognize that my life is not my own
That Jesus paid the price
He shed his blood
And grace abounds

Now my life is totally committed
To serving You
Pleasing You
My life is totally committed
To doing all You would have me to do
Being all You want me to be
Your vessel

So, what would You have me to do today
What word shall I speak
What path should I take
What would You have me to do

Come

Come my friend
Give me your hand
Our time is short
Can you not feel it?
Just as quick as you blink a day has passed
The times are frightening
People are loosing jobs and hope
The earth shows its disgust
With rumblings, fire, and ash

I must insist you come
I hear of another war breaking out
I know a place of safety where you may rest
You don't have time to pack
You must leave all your bags behind
The weight will hinder your travel to the gates

Come-don't worry about food, clothes, or shelter
All preparations have been made for our destination
As well as our journey

Come—now is the time

He Kissed Me

Take my hand and come with me
I may not be here tomorrow to show you the way
Each day the gates move closer together
Making the way even more narrow

Come—before the trumpet sounds
And the gates close
Come—incline your ear
Take my hand and live

Expectation
(Jeremiah 29:11)

10
Wow! Another year is passing
9
At least I am still here
8
A year filled with joy and sorrow—just where did it go
7
I accomplished some things and other things just never got off the ground
6
I am still not where I think I should be
5
But I am still here
4
That means another chance
3
To achieve
2
To believe in the only
1

Prepare Me

Prepare me
Prepare me Lord
To be with You

The day is coming when You will return for me
To take me away from all iniquity
It is my desire to be what You would have me to be

Prepare me to be with You

That I may stand before You in all Your glory
See Your loving face
Hold out my hand and feel Your warm embrace
Hear Your tender words of love
It is my desire to be near You

Prepare me
Prepare me Lord
To be with You

The day is coming when I will be with You
When what You have waited for

Perfection
Will reign

No longer will I thirst
Nor will sadness come against me
And heat shall not prevail

I just ask that You
Prepare me
To be with You

Another Level

Press, move, push
Move, push
Press

I feel the spirit of the Lord all around me

Move

Love just flowing
I feel the spirit of the Lord encamped about me

Push

Fighting my battles

If I can just continue to press my way
    The reward shall be mine
If I can just continue to move upon the word of God
    Eternal life is mine
If I can just continue to push-the battles already won

I feel the spirit-moving
I feel the spirit of the Lord—moving, moving

I've got to press, move, push, move, push
Press my way
I've got to press, move, push, move, push
Press my way

Higher Praise
Higher Love
Higher Worship
Higher, Higher
High le lu jah!
Hallelujah, hallelujah
Hallelujah!

I've Come Too Far

I know you have your lackeys keeping watch over me
Reporting to you the effect you have on me
But I've come too far
To allow you to run over me
To dictate how I feel
NO!
My Father told me to resist you
You must flee
Oh, you try
Situations arise and problems come my way
But you must have forgotten who's child I am
Despite those things
I'm going to bless the Lord
With all my soul
And every last drop within me
I shall cry out Hallelujah
And break the barriers you've placed
They must come down
They can't stand against the Living God
So send your lackeys

Try to keep me down
But I've come too far
To forfeit the victory I've already won

Use Me

Steadfast and free as the wind
Your presence moves me
Shaking the ground beneath me
To jar my soul
I hear, my Lord
I hear
And here I stand
Your vessel on this earth

Strong, true, and far reaching
As the branches of a mighty tree
You have stretched out your hand
And I have grabbed hold
Use me, my Lord
Use me

Got To Tell It (The News)

Psst. Psst.
Over here.
Pssssssst. Bend your ear this way.
News Flash: Important Life Saving News:
Good News Is Headed Your Way . . . .
. . . . Jesus Is Alive!!!!!

Listen—Then Go

After a weekend of praise and exaltation
Declaring, "Lord, I'll go. Send me."
I send to you a defeated co-worker
In need of a word of love
A thread of hope
But because of the package in which it was sent
You see only what your flesh will allow
Sin, filth, unrighteousness
What happened?
Did I not command you to preach,
"The kingdom of heaven is at hand?"

At home, a family member is ill
Do you seek Me for healing?
Break out the oil and lay hands upon them?
You have the power to heal the sick
Cleanse the leper
But this power is wasted away

Have I not left word for devils to be cast out?
Why are so many of my people bound?
Because you are bond

Shake yourself from the dust
Wake up and come before Me
With a repented heart
Stay broken before Me
And remove the bands from your neck

I need you to be free
To preach My Word
Heal My sick
Cleanse My lepers
Cast out those devils

I need you to freely give Me to the world
In spite of the package it is wrapped in
Look beyond the outward appearance
See the softening of the heart

Fear not for I have redeemed you
Called you by name
You are Mine
I will not let go

If you have an ear to hear, listen

When I say "Go!"
Know that the path has been prepared

When I say "Go!"
Look not at the mountains about you

I have given you the power of faith
Remove them

When I say "Go!"
Realize that you can not go unless I send you
If I have sent you
You do not operate out of self
But it is **My power, My might, My authority**
That works through you

When I say "Go!"
Know that you are My witness
My servant
Whom I have chosen
You are My witness that I am God

Do you have ears to hear?
Are you listening?

GO!